Marine Marvels

Contents	Page

written by Rachel Walker

The seas of the world are home to many unusual creatures –
providing them with the food and shelter they need to survive.
The main types of marine animals that we know are reptiles,
mammals, crustaceans and fish.

Marine reptiles include sea turtles, sea snakes, marine iguanas,
and saltwater crocodiles.

All reptiles:

- have scaly skin
- lay eggs
- are cold blooded (except for the leatherback sea turtle).

marine iguana

A sea turtle spends most of its life at sea. After hatching on beaches, males never return to land at all. In summer the females come up on beaches at night for a brief hour to make nests, lay eggs, and bury them in the sand, where they are left to develop and hatch. After about two months, the baby turtles tear their shells apart with their snouts, dig out through the sand, and scuttle across the beach to the sea.

sea turtle

Saltwater crocodiles
are the largest
of all the living
crocodile species
in the world. They
normally swim very
slowly, but they can
move with a sudden
burst of speed
when attacking.
Saltwater crocs like
to feed on other
reptiles, small
mammals, fish and
crustaceans. Even
sharks can fall
prey to these huge
crocodiles!

There are 4 major groups of marine mammals:

1. Cetaceans – whales, dolphins and porpoises.
2. Pinnipeds – seals, sea lions and walruses.
3. Fissipeds – polar bears and sea otters.
4. Sirenians – manatees and dugongs (sea cows).

All mammals:
- give birth to live young
- produce milk to feed their babies
- are warm-blooded
- breathe air.

dugong

beluga whale

Sea mammals such as whales and dolphins come to the surface at regular intervals to breathe through the "blowhole" on the top of the head. When they breathe air out through the blowhole it is seen as spray called a spout. After they breathe air in, the blowhole is closed by a flap to stop water from getting into the lungs.

Polar bears spend most of their lives in icy Arctic seas, where their slightly webbed toes help them to swim powerfully. They have coarse, hollow fur that traps heat close to their bodies, helping them to survive in their extreme habitat that includes land, sea, snow and ice.

Crustaceans include lobsters, crabs, shrimps and barnacles.
All crustaceans:

- have a hard crusty shell that they outgrow and then replace
  (by growing a new one)
- have two pairs of antennae
- lay eggs
- have many pairs of jointed legs.

Fish dominate the waters of our planet, with over 25,000 different species in the world. All fish have gills through which they breathe oxygen directly from the water.

The 3 major groups of fish are:

1. Bony fish – most species.
2. Jawless fish – primitive, sucking mouthparts.
3. Invertebrates/Cartilaginous fish – sharks, jellyfish and rays.

Invertebrates are a type of fish with no bones. Instead, their bodies are supported by cartilage, just like the cartilage humans have in the tip of the nose. Jellyfish are invertebrates with tentacles that can sting. All jellyfish sting – some dangerously – but the stings of small specimens and those with short tentacles are not often painful to humans.

Sharks are invertebrates with more than 400 different species. An unusual shark is the Hammerhead, which has eyes and nostrils at both ends of its hammer-shaped head. This position of its eyes allows full-circle vision. Hammerhead sharks hunt alone at night, feeding mainly on fish and squid. Unlike many fish, hammerhead sharks do not lay eggs – instead, the female gives birth to live young. One litter can range from 6 to about 50 pups!

There are at least 25 species of seahorses in the world's tropical and temperate coastal waters, swimming upright among seaweed and other plants. Seahorses are tiny fish that use camouflage to match their surroundings if an enemy appears. They can twist their tails around coral or seaweed to anchor themselves while they feed on tiny prey floating by. A female seahorse lays dozens (sometimes hundreds!) of eggs, which she gives to the male seahorse to carry in a special brood pouch until they hatch.

Now, as modern technology develops, marine scientists are using diving machines called submersibles to take them to deep unexplored parts of the oceans. There, divers are discovering undersea creatures that have never been seen by humans before. Who knows what wonderful and unusual marine marvels will be discovered next?